THE PRODIGAL FATHERS

"Nigerian Leaders, Come to Your Senses!
Stop Squandering Our Commonwealth" ...
Voice of the Suffering Masses

Iyke Temple Nwabueze

CONTENTS

INTRODUCTION

The Prodigal Path of Nigerian Leadership

For too long, the masses of Nigeria have cried out, suffering under the weight of their leaders' prodigal actions. The revelation of unchecked corruption, mind-boggling misallocation of resources, and an utter disregard for the public welfare has left the nation's immense potential scandalously unrealized.

Like the biblical prodigal son who abandoned his inheritance through reckless living, Nigeria's prodigal fathers have squandered the nation's vast wealth and opportunities entrusted to them. They have indulged their own excesses, enriching themselves and their associates while the majority of citizens wallow in preventable poverty.

The evidence is overwhelming - the billions upon billions allegedly looted and ferreted away to private accounts and foreign lands. The "white elephant" projects greenlighted more for their graft-enabling largesse than any public benefit. The piling up of debt upon debt to fund unsustainable spending rather than productive investment. This path of prodigality has bankrupted not just the public coffers but the very promise of Nigeria.

Crumbling infrastructure, a failing educational system, inadequate healthcare, environmental degradation - the legacy of prodigal rule has shortchanged and betrayed succeeding generations of Nigerians. Economic growth and development has stagnated as the resources to power transformation are siphoned into private pockets.

The costs of this prodigality are not just financial but moral. Trust in democracy, good governance, and ethical leadership has been decimated by repeated revelations of brazen dishonesty and impropriety from those who repeatedly take Sworn oaths to uphold the public trust only to violate them with impunity.

This book is a clarion call - to current and future leaders of Nigeria, to reject the prodigal path that has inflicted such damage and despair upon the masses. It outlines the ethical, pragmatic and economic imperative of embracing the values of discipline, accountability and selflessness in leadership.

The way forward requires an upheaval of the status quo, a revolution that empowers citizens and enforces open, participatory governance. It calls upon those who would lead to respect and judiciously harness Nigeria's wealth and potential for the benefit of the entire nation and future generations to come.

No longer can Nigeria's long-suffering people abide the wanton prodigality that has scattered the nation's inheritance upon the trail of corruption and indiscipline. The time has come for prodigal fathers to be redeemed, to return to the principles of integrity, and to rededicate themselves to serving as faithful stewards of the Commonwealth entrusted to them.

For only once prodigality is rejected and good governance embraced, can Nigeria and its people finally rise to their true destiny as a proud, prosperous, powerful nation. The path will not be easy, but it is the only way to escape the destitution born of prodigality and realize the greatness within reach.

CHAPTER 1 -

Squandering the Nation's Wealth

- Historical examples of misuse of public funds
- White elephant projects draining resources
- Excessive corruption and embezzlement

CHAPTER 2 –

The Plundered Commonwealth

- Impact of prodigal spending on development
- Lacking infrastructure, health, and education
- Rising poverty and inequality among the masses

CHAPTER 3 –

Betrayal of the Public Trust

- Reckless accumulation of national debt
- Self-enrichment over service to the people
- Undermining of democratic principles

CHAPTER 4 -

A Cry From the Suffering Masses

- Voices from impoverished communities
- Hopes and dreams betrayed by failed leadership
- Demand for accountability and change

CHAPTER 5 -

Rejecting the Prodigal Way

- Examples of principled leaders prioritizing nation
- The moral and pragmatic case against prodigality
- Virtues of frugality, investment, sustainability

CHAPTER 6 -

Transparency: The Light to Reform

- **Institutionalizing openness and public oversight**
- **Citizen participation and empowerment**
- **Technologies increasing accountability**

CHAPTER 7 -

Good Governance: The Antidote

- Anti-corruption initiatives and enforcement
- Civil service commitment to public good
- Prudent management of national resources

CHAPTER 8 -

A Prosperous Future Reclaimed

- Potential realized through governance reform
- Funding human capital and economic development
- Restoring faith in the Nigerian dream

Conclusion -

An Ethical Revolution for Transformation

- Final call to Nigerian leaders to reject prodigality
- Embracing discipline and selflessness in leadership
- Becoming fathers of a proud, powerful nation

Appendix: 1 –

Case Studies and Success Stories Exemplary Leaders: Lessons from Past and Present

Appendix: 2 –

Case Studies and Success Stories Exemplary Nigerian Leaders: Lessons from Past and Present

Appendix: 3 –

Case Studies and Success Stories Grassroots Initiatives: Inspiring Change from the Bottom Up

References: –

Citations

Recommended Further Reading

INTRODUCTION -

The Prodigal Path of Nigerian Leadership

For too long, the masses of Nigeria have cried out, suffering under the weight of their leaders' prodigal actions. The revelation of unchecked corruption, mind-boggling misallocation of resources, and an utter disregard for the public welfare has left the nation's immense potential scandalously unrealized.

Like the biblical prodigal son who abandoned his inheritance through reckless living, Nigeria's prodigal fathers have squandered the nation's vast wealth and opportunities entrusted to them. They have indulged their own excesses, enriching themselves and their associates while the majority of citizens wallow in preventable poverty.

The evidence is overwhelming - the billions upon billions allegedly looted and ferreted away to private accounts and foreign lands. The "white elephant" projects greenlighted more for their graft-enabling largesse than any public benefit. The piling up of debt upon debt to fund unsustainable spending rather than productive investment. This path of prodigality has bankrupted not just the public coffers but the very promise of Nigeria.

Crumbling infrastructure, a failing educational system, inadequate healthcare, environmental degradation - the legacy of prodigal rule has shortchanged and betrayed succeeding generations of Nigerians. Economic growth and development has stagnated as the resources to power transformation are siphoned into private pockets.

The costs of this prodigality are not just financial but moral. Trust in democracy, good governance, and ethical leadership has been decimated by repeated revelations of brazen dishonesty and impropriety from those who repeatedly take Sworn oaths to uphold the public trust only to violate them with impunity.

This book is a clarion call - to current and future leaders of Nigeria, to reject the prodigal path that has inflicted such damage and despair upon the masses. It outlines the ethical, pragmatic and economic imperative of embracing the values of discipline, accountability and selflessness in leadership.

The way forward requires an upheaval of the status quo, a revolution that empowers citizens and enforces open, participatory governance. It calls upon those who would lead to respect and judiciously harness Nigeria's wealth and potential for the benefit of the entire nation and future generations to come.

No longer can Nigeria's long-suffering people abide the wanton prodigality that has scattered the nation's inheritance upon the trail of corruption and indiscipline. The time has come for prodigal fathers to be redeemed, to return to the principles of integrity, and to rededicate themselves to serving as faithful stewards of the Commonwealth entrusted to them.

For only once prodigality is rejected and good governance embraced, can Nigeria and its people finally rise to their true destiny as a proud, prosperous, powerful nation. The path will not be easy, but it is the only way to escape the destitution born of prodigality and realize the greatness within reach.

CHAPTER 1 -

Squandering the Nation's Wealth

Historical examples of misuse of public funds

The prodigal misspending of Nigeria's resources and corrosive misallocation of public funds is a crisis that has spanned administrations and decades. Almost since independence, the control of the nation's oil wealth and revenues has been a corrupting influence on governance.

In the 1970s and 80s, the Shagari and Buhari regimes oversaw the accumulation of over $30 billion in external debt through fiscal indiscipline and white elephant projects like the Ajaokuta Steel Plant that swallowed billions with no sustainable benefit. The notoriously corrupt Abacha military dictatorship in the 1990s witnessed the broad pillaging of state coffers - over $5 billion was discovered to have been looted directly into Abacha's personal accounts abroad.

More recently, the Obasanjo civilian administration claimed recoveries of $2.7 billion in looted funds repatriated from foreign havens. However, over $10 billion was squandered on an ill-conceived National Integrated Power Project that made only marginal improvements to the electricity sector after years of mismanagement.

The alleged diversion of $20 billion in security funds meant to equip the military and combat Boko Haram during the Goodluck Jonathan presidency highlights how funds desperately needed for vital priorities are prodigally siphoned away from their purpose.

White elephant projects draining resources

A signature of Nigeria's prodigal leadership has been the propensity for initiating and funding grandiose vanity projects and infrastructure that is often unnecessary, poorly conceived, and deprioritizes more urgent public needs.

The excessive funds poured into building the Abuja Capital City and its lavish buildings like the N64 billion Centenary City stand in stark contrast to the decrepit state of education, healthcare, and basic services in much of the country. The Aso Rock Presidential Complex, occupying over 10 square kilometers, epitomizes the prodigal instinct for unwieldy and costly "white elephant" projects.

Ill-conceived initiatives like the $8.3 billion Kaduna pipeline project, the $12 billion Mambilla Power Station, and the $18 billion proposal for a new capital city have made continuous drains on scarce funding while yielding minimal public benefit and development impact. Too many times, prodigal prestige projects trump investing in urgently needed public goods like hospitals, roads, and schools.

Excessive corruption and embezzlement

At the root cause of the prodigal squandering of Nigeria's wealth, potential, and future is the crippling chronic issue of corruption. As funds allocated for public development projects get siphoned off illegally into private pockets, the nation's resources perpetually bleed away.

Not only does large-scale embezzlement of state funds directly deplete resources, but the edifice of corruption itself creates hefty economic drags. Bribery and fraud impose dead weight costs that deter investment. Funds that could catalyze growth are diverted into illicit private gains. Talented professionals, despairing of corruption's stranglehold, take their skills abroad in "brain drains" that further hamstring development.

Estimates by watchdog groups have alleged that as much as $20 billion may have been embezzled from public coffers during the decade of the 2000s alone. With corruption ingrained from the highest levels down to the lowest state contractors, the theft of the nation's commonwealth occurs as a ruthless draining of funds meant to uplift society.

This chronic embezzlement is the most egregious and unforgivable form of prodigal excess - the wholesale theft of the people's inheritance by their own entrusted leaders and representatives. It is a depraved prodigality that must be rooted out for any transformation to take root.

CHAPTER 2 –

The Plundered Commonwealth

Impact of prodigal spending on development

The generational impacts of prodigal governance and resource squandering in Nigeria have been utterly devastating for the nation's development potential. What could have been a prosperous petro-economy leveraging its oil revenues to build a diverse and resilient industrial base has instead stagnated under the weight of misallocation and mismanagement.

With an enormous percentage of the government's budget expenditure diverted to bloated overhead costs, inflated contracts, and graft-laden boondoggles, the funding available for true investment in development initiatives has been pitifully inadequate. Just a fraction of oil revenues have flowed into building human capital, catalyzing economic diversification, or financing public goods and infrastructure that create productivity gains.

The consequences are evident in Nigeria's poor rankings on development metrics compared to its resource wealth and potential. Deficiencies in infrastructure like reliable power, transportation, and telecoms cost the economy an estimated 3% annually in forgone GDP growth. The manufacturing and agriculture sectors that should be engines of jobs and exports remain undercapitalized.

Rather than economic transformation, the prodigal spending priorities of successive administrations have condemned the economy to being a mere rentier state over-dependent on the whims of oil prices and production rather than diversified, value-adding industries.

Lacking infrastructure, health, and education

With so much of the nation's resource wealth squandered prodigally rather than invested prudently in development foundations, the impacts on social infrastructure like health, education, and basic services has been calamitous for millions of Nigerians.

In the education sector, public funding has been abysmal, crippling the quality of instruction, learner retention, and education outcomes. With over 13 million children out of school, betrayed of their human capital potentials, entire generations are effectively sacrificed to ignorance and diminished opportunities.

Healthcare has similarly suffered from decades of systematic defunding and neglect amid prodigal plundering. Just 3.9% of GDP is devoted to health expenditures, among the lowest levels globally. Dilapidated facilities, shortages of medicines and equipment, and a dearth of medical professionals make quality care unaffordable for most Nigerians.

For basic infrastructure, the failings are omnipresent - municipalities struggle to maintain potable water systems; over half the population lacks access to improved sanitation; electricity provision remains erratic and undependable. These deficiencies impose immense social costs and degrade the dignity and quality of life for society.

Rising poverty and inequality among the masses

As the prodigal raiding of Nigeria's commonwealth has diverted resources from development, the consequences have manifested most cruelly in rising mass impoverishment and worsening inequality nationwide. Despite possessing vast oil wealth, over 40% of the population subsists in extreme poverty at levels worse than significantly less resource-rich nations.

Income inequality has soared in tandem, a sure sign of the mal-distribution of economic opportunity and benefits caused by prodigal misgovernance. Rather than uplifting the masses, the squandering of the nation's riches has consigned the majority to destitution.

Such systemic impoverishment spawns a negative feedback loop that further inhibits development progress – malnourishment and health deficiencies reduce workforce productivity; lack of educational access hamstrings human capital development; deficient infrastructure raises operating costs for businesses and makes the nation globally uncompetitive.

Ultimately, the persistently high poverty rates are generational sentences of diminished social mobility, hope, and human potentials for swathes of Nigerians. This travesty is made all the more bitter by the wanton prodigality that has diverted and siphoned away resources that could power real economic empowerment of the masses.

When a nation's immense wealth becomes so monopolized by prodigal leadership to the detriment of the populace, the social fabric is severely ruptured. Such is the tragedy of the plundered Nigerian commonwealth at the hands of prodigal fathers prioritizing personal enrichment over public welfare.

CHAPTER 3 –

Betrayal of the Public Trust

Reckless accumulation of national debt

A signature symptom and perpetuating cause of Nigeria's prodigal governance has been the reckless, unsustainable accumulation of national debt undertaken with brazen disregard for future costs or economic impacts. Profligate spending not undergirded by productive investment has mortgaged the nation's prospects to spiraling debt service obligations.

Under the weight of prodigality, Nigeria's external debt ballooned from just $3.6 billion in 1985 to over $36 billion by 2004 before securing some relief. However, debt levels began their inexorable rise again, doubling to $77 billion by 2020 as funds were siphoned away from genuine development expenditures.

This has created a perpetual debt trap - approximately 60% of government revenues now must be devoted to interest payments rather than investing in diversifying the economy and weaning the nation from its debt addiction. With China now Nigeria's single largest creditor, fears mount that prodigal debt dependencies could compromise national policy sovereignty.

Such reckless, unproductive debt accumulation is an acute betrayal of the public trust. Rather than spending judiciously within their means, prodigal administrations have effectively hijacked Nigeria's economic future, shackling generations of citizens to liabilities glutted by graft rather than invested for sustainable prosperity.

Self-enrichment over service to the people

At the dark core driving Nigeria's prodigal governance crisis is the endemic prioritization of self-interest and personal enrichment by officials over any true commitment to public service. Rather than being faithful stewards safeguarding the commonwealth, an entrenched ethos of extractive, rent-seeking behavior has pulverized integrity in public institutions.

Whether it's the $3 billion seized from the associates of former military ruler Abacha, the unexplained wealth of former governors like James Ibori, or the countless scandals involving inflated contracts and bribery - the modus operandi has become funneling public resources into private reservoirs of illicit wealth and luxury.

This banality of unchecked greed has corroded any conception of public offices being a public trust. Lacking accountability, morality, or shame, the prodigal plunder of national resources gets subsumed as normalcy rather than criminality in the popular conscience.

Such depths of ethical bankruptcy impose massive deadweight costs on the entire society and development trajectory. Why strive for good governance when bad governance so lucratively rewards the perpetrators? How can effective institutions take root when the incentive structure is rigged for parasitic extraction rather than promoting the public good?

Until this culture of unconstrained self-dealing is systematically upended, the betrayal of the Nigerian public's trust and inherited resources shall only continue unabated at the hands of prodigal leaderships prioritizing themselves over the nation.

Undermining of democratic principles

Beyond just the financial costs of prodigality, the systemic effects have gravely undermined core democratic principles of accountability, transparency, rule of law, and representation of the citizenry's interests that must underpin any truly legitimate governance system.

With the unbridled ability to loot and misappropriate funds at their personal discretion, Nigeria's elected executives at national and state levels have effectively converted their powers into kleptocratic fiefdoms. Public mandates get supplanted by structures facilitating graft and clientelism, eroding any real democratic accountability.

An obscene climate of impunity has taken hold, as prodigal overindulgence evades consequences amid compromised oversight institutions and law enforcement. The perpetrators are effectively "too wealthy to jail", spreading cynicism about the lack of equality under the law. Injustice begets injustice.

Furthermore, the perpetuation of prodigal governance has systematically stripped Nigerians of their democratic voices, empowering them in name only. With resources prodigally diverted from public goods, citizens become subjugated, their human capital imprisoned by degraded schools and services. Poverty disempowers, making meaningless ballots unaccompanied by economic rights.

In essence, the prodigal scourge has hollowed out Nigerian democracy to a mere facade masking self-perpetuating apparatuses of extraction and marginalization of the masses. Redressing this subversion of democratic legitimacy is a fight for the sanctity of the social contract itself - to reclaim the commonwealth from prodigal plunder.

CHAPTER 4 –

A Cry From the Suffering Masses

Voices from impoverished communities

To fully grasp the human toll of prodigal governance in Nigeria, one must listen to the voices crying out from the nation's most impoverished and marginalized communities. It is here where the generational betrayal by failed, self-serving leadership has reaped its cruelest consequences.

In the Niger Delta, where billions have been squandered amid endemic corporate and bureaucratic greed, communities like Ogoni lament being made to survive amid environmental degradation, malnutrition, and entrenched poverty while the oil wealth on their lands fuels such prodigality.

"Our children are being poisoned by the polluted lands and waters," laments one village elder, "yet our royalties and assistance funds all disappear into private pockets of the corrupt."

In the agrarian heart of the nation, where subsistence farmers merely try to eke out meager existences, villages decry the systemic neglect by prodigal state and local governments. "Our schools have no books, no toilets. Our clinics have no doctors, no medicines," voices rise. "Our only road washes out each rainy season as our paramount needs go unmet."

From the sprawling urban slums and shantytowns, where millions endure daily indignities of squalor amid the nation's vast energy riches, outcries for justice and accountability only amplify. "We have no lights, no clean water. We risk our lives obtaining these basics while they build mansions from the wealth under our feet."

These anguished lived realities, replicated in communities across Nigeria's breadth, attest to the scale of deprivation, despair, anger and resentment sowed by the unbridled prodigality of the nation's leadership vis-a-vis the suffering masses.

Hopes and dreams betrayed by failed leadership

At the core of the disillusionment pervading impoverished sectors of Nigerian society is the shattered hope that democratic rule would finally align their long-abused nation's trajectory with their interests and aspirations for better lives. After enduring decades of oppressive military misrule, the democratic revival stoked dreams of equitable distribution of the national wealth. Yet prodigal leadership perpetuated the patterns of elite rent capture.

"We celebrated having a real voice again only to be forgotten, sacrificed so they could personally benefit from the oil riches," rues a local activist in Port Harcourt. With each successive scandal involving looted billions meant for development, such dashed hopes have calcified into resignation that democracy has merely ushered new versions of systemic marginalization.

In the youth demographics, where joblessness and lack of economic prospects beset over 60% of under-35s nationwide, impatience with the prodigal status quo has fueled militancy, unrest, and brain drains robbing Nigeria of its future:

"We studied, we voted, but they keep rigging the system to ensure the looting never gets upended. So we burn buildings. We join rebels. We look abroad for existence - because here is just the same old prodigal fathers devouring our futures."

Such decaying of faith in the ethical renovating promise of democracy, in the ideals of a sober and fair leadership class governing for collective nation-building, has bred a simmering cynicism. It is a malignant resignation that facilitates the dehumanization of the masses into passive bystanders to the prodigality plundering their commonwealth.

Demand for accountability and change

Yet amid this sea of profound betrayal by prodigal governance, the resilient defiance of the impoverished Nigerian masses still cries out in collective, unified demand for long-overdue accountability and transformational change. From grassroots protest movements to youth activists embracing new technologies, a clamor rises to finally upend the systemic detachment of leadership from the will and welfare of the people.

"We have survived their unconscionable neglect for so long, they think we've resigned," declares one community organizer from Lagos. "But now, armed with social media to raise our voices in unison, we demand to finally be represented - not pillaged."

Whether it's citizen video documentation of abandoned public projects gone awry or viral pushback campaigns against revealed looting scandals, a participatory grassroots is coalescing to expose the depths of the prodigal plunder and its perpetrators. The specter of accountability and consequences seems ever more palpable.

"We cannot be divided and silenced any longer," affirms one forceful youth activist voice. "They have thwarted democracy's promise through their prodigal thievery for too long. So we brace to uproot it - withholding our critical labor, our civic energies, our fealties - until this path of prodigal governance is abolished. We want our nation reborn, with ethical leadership, investment in our futures, equitable dignity for all."

From the groundswell of anguished masses yearning to be served rather than plundered by their governors, a transformational reckoning may finally be brewing. The cry has gone up - to reject the prodigal path is to pursue the sole remaining hope for a redeemed, prosperous Nigeria.

CHAPTER 5 -

Rejecting the Prodigal Way

Examples of principled leaders prioritizing nation

Though the plague of prodigal leadership has indelibly marred Nigeria's postcolonial experience, the nation has witnessed inspiring examples of principled public stewardship that reveal an alternative could be possible. These countervailing models of integrity over self-interest provide a blueprint for how transformative governance can take root.

One of the most celebrated examples is that of former President Murtala Mohammed, whose brief 1975-1976 tenure instituted ethical reforms to combat Nigerian's already metastasizing corruption. He fired hundreds of public officials, centralized revenue collection away from rent-seeking, and prescribed execution for any further purveyors of graft, warning bluntly: "Any elementary teacher who cannot explain to pupils what he earns his wages for is a swindler."

Mohammed's Spartan personal integrity stood in stark rebuke to the prodigal excess pervading past and future administrations. Never taking bribes or abusing public resources, he governed through an ethos of hard work, austerity, and service to the people. Tragically assassinated, his vision of an accountable, productive Nigeria governed by moral compasses rather than proclivity for plunder proved ephemeral.

A later seminal figure was Nuhu Ribadu, who as Nigeria's first internationally-trained financial crimes prosecutor, spearheaded

economy have cost Nigeria billions in forgone growth and deterred over $10 billion annually in foreign investment due to endemic graft risks.

Furthermore, the accumulated debts from decades of prodigal fiscal incontinence now leave Nigeria devoting over 60% of revenues to debt service rather than productive spending on infrastructure, human capital, and diversifying the economic base beyond extractive industries. This makes the nation extremely vulnerable to external shocks like oil price volatility.

In essence, prodigality begets underdevelopment, locking Nigeria into a perpetual underperformer status relative to its resource endowments. The poverty, inequality, brain drains, poor public services, and institutional weaknesses born of the resource curse feedback loop only further erode economic foundations. Governance failures compound into compounded human insecurities.

It is this vicious, self-reinforcing cycle that urgently demands sweeping systemic reforms to eliminate the perverse incentives and enabling environments facilitating prodigal practices. Good governance aimed at catalyzing investment, sustainable public financial management, anticorruption enforcement, and transparency is not just a moral nicety. It is Nigeria's lone remaining hope for survival, security, and restored potential as a prosperous democratic nation able to provide for its masses.

Simply put, continuing to tolerate the entrenched prodigality will only accelerate Nigeria's descent towards state failure. Rejecting it by institutionalizing accountability and prudent economic stewardship from the highest echelons down to local oversight is now an existential priority. The moral and pragmatic rationales are unified.

Virtues of frugality, investment, sustainability

In stark contradistinction to the endemic wastefulness,

embezzlement, and myopic squandering enabled by Nigeria's legacy of prodigal governance, the ethical leadership principles that must be embraced emphasize the core virtues of frugality, strategic investment, and sustainability as the surest path to robust economic development and human security.

Frugality demands embracing moderation, needs-based allocation of resources, and a culture of austerity and prudence in public expenditures after decades of profligacy and mismanagement. State institutions must be redesigned to cap excessive bureaucratic bloat and curb rent-seeking vulnerabilities that enabled abuse, from military spending to civil service compensation levels.

This frugality then creates fiscal space to prioritize and ramp up productive investments in physical and human capital foundations for sustainable, diversified growth that crowds in private development. Funding for education, healthcare, critical infrastructure, agriculture, manufacturing, and technological upskilling must be protected and increased from their perennial deprioritization under prodigal administrations.

Just as important as the investment priorities are the sustainability principles emphasizing careful resource husbandry, generational equity, and economic resiliency against external shocks like oil dependence. Too often, capital project plans or fiscal policies were shaped by short-term boons of windfalls or debt booms under the prodigal model.

A sustainability ethos would seek to preserve and grow Nigeria's national wealth through judicious, countercyclical revenue management and development of sovereign wealth funds to insulate budgets from volatility. Rather than perpetually mortgaging the future, this protects the inherited resources of future generations through inter-generational investment returns.

Success would be marked by steadily improving public

goods provision, rising human development metrics, and economic diversification away from excessive reliance on extractives. Sustainability envisions a Nigeria resilient to shocks, economically durable through prudent capital accumulation and avoidance of the perpetual boom-bust cycles enabled by prodigal policymaking.

In sum, these virtues of frugality, investment, and sustainability represent the antithesis of the wanton resource squandering and embezzlement that has marred Nigeria under the prodigal era. Embracing them will demand transcending decades of ethical decay and rebuilding public institutions with citizen vigilance. But the transformation unlocked presents Nigeria's best, and perhaps last, chance to recover its destiny as a prosperous, stable, secure democratic state.

CHAPTER 6 -

Transparency: The Light to Reform

Institutionalizing openness and public oversight

Any genuine reform effort to redeem Nigeria from the cycle of prodigal plundering must enshrine transparency as a core operating principle across all facets of governance. Decades of opaque management of public finances and economic activities have enabled the festering of unchecked corruption and abuse of office for private gain. Sunlight must become the disinfectant.

Instituting transparency requires systematic initiatives and legal frameworks compelling openness about government budgets, contracting, resource revenue flows, fiscal decisions and expenditures. From the national level down to states and localities, budget and spending information should be accessible public information, with independent audits and oversight mandated.

Key economic data like extractive industry payments, sovereign wealth fund account balances, debt management records, and investment policies must similarly transition to being open access, with public participation in monitoring. Too long have these information asymmetries enabled gluttonous pilfering in the dark.

Furthermore, transparency also extends to compelling asset declarations and disclosures of potential conflicts of interest across public officials overseeing state commercial relations and projects. Making these declaratory regimes strictly enforced institutionalizes deterrents against influence peddling and self-dealing that pervade Nigeria's prodigal governance landscape.

Critically, transparency requires robust protections for whistleblowers, anti-corruption activists, and a free press able to investigate and expose kleptocratic schemes unconstrained. An informed citizenry empowered to scrutinize and raise accountability demands can revolutionize the ability to dismantle cultures of graft.

Critically, transparency reforms must be constitutionally enshrined with powerful independent oversight bodies insulated from partisan interference or retaliation by those threatened with consequences for illicit financial activities. Building an enduring legacy of openness provides the critical foundations to make transformative change irreversible.

Citizen participation and empowerment

For too long, the disenfranchised masses of Nigeria have been shut out as passive beneficiaries from their nation's resource wealth and economic governance with no substantive voice or role. A core pillar of upending the prodigal system must be empowering citizens with real participatory mechanisms in directing resource allocation priorities and oversight roles.

On the local level, this means devolving more fiscal decision-making to community development committees and municipal authorities with open town halls and participatory budgeting models. The people most reliant upon public services should have direct say in prioritizing expenditures rather than having funds captured by patronage networks.

Civil society groups and grassroots activists must be integrated as indispensable partners across levels, serving on oversight boards and as statutory public watchdogs empowered to scrutinize and uphold transparency standards. Public consultations and open feedback loops become mandated for major projects and policies.

At national levels, the populace deserves avenues like public referenda to weigh in on major natural resource decisions like extractives concessions. Codified buffers against executive unilateralism on issues impacting national patrimony. Citizen empowerment is not about gridlock, it's about ownership and enforcing accountability to prevent resource hijacking.

Combined with expansive rights to information, ethics trainings, social audits and participatory expenditure monitoring, this integration of the grassroots into governance evolves Nigeria into a system of public resource stewardship. It transforms subjects of neglected development into economic stakeholders with empowered voices.

When coupled with transparency mechanisms providing visibility into official financial activities, avenues for citizen oversight can permanently disrupt the opacity and cultures of impunity that enabled generations of prodigal looting under Nigerian's rent-seeking political economy status quo.

Technologies increasing accountability

Leveraging Nigeria's growing technological infrastructure and innovation ecosystem can provide pivotal new tools to deepen transparency and empower citizens with accountability oversight. Nationwide digital platforms and data analytics capabilities have immense potential to systematically disincentivize rent extraction while engaging the public.

Initiatives like Nigeria's Open Treasury and Open Contracting data portals are already beginning to put comprehensive expenditure databases online. Coupled with data mining capabilities, granular tracking can illuminate discrepancies, vendor risks, and contract inflation in ways fostering accountability.

Digitization also enables transforming convoluted paper-based processes for revenue accounting and payrolls into centralized e-governance systems hardened against fraud and pilfering leakages. Secure digital identities and digital payments can curb graft in disbursement channels.

As IT infrastructure spreads like Nigeria's identity database system and rural connectivity, emerging possibilities like distributed ledgers or blockchain databases can further decentralize and encrypt records in immutable public ledgers impervious to manipulation by officials.

Furthermore, purposefully designing feedback loops for crowdsourced reporting of grievances, tracking service delivery, or documenting corruption creates powerful citizen engagement and monitoring capabilities. From SMS reporting hotlines to online platforms, the populace gains tools to shine light into opaque corners.

When reinforced with strong public access laws and protections for whistleblowers, journalists, and anti-corruption activists, new technologies can shift the power asymmetries long favoring those benefiting from Nigeria's extractive, elite-dominated systems.

Ultimately, the reinvigorated transparency, accountability feedback loops, and citizen empowerment enabled by digital governance innovation reconfigures incentives in favor of public servants prioritizing real development outcomes over illicit private enrichment. It can catalyze a new equilibrium transcending the entrenched legacies of Nigeria's prodigal status quo.

CHAPTER 7 -

Good Governance: The Antidote

Anti-corruption initiatives and enforcement

At the core of extinguishing Nigeria's crippling crisis of prodigal governance lies the pressing imperative to dismantle the systemic apparatus enabling corruption and illicit self-enrichment with public resources. Too long has graft been the operative norm rather than an aberration. Decisive anti-corruption initiatives backed by rigorous enforcement and adjudication must become institutionalized at all levels.

First, effective asset recovery and anti-money laundering regimes are urgently needed to deprive corrupt actors of their criminal proceeds while deterring the bank secrecy enabling global havenization of Nigeria's looted wealth. Eliminating incentives through aggressive enforcement of asset seizures and repatriations is critical.

Within Nigeria's judicial system, dedicated anti-graft courts and elite prosecutorial teams focused on financial crimes must be insulated from political interference and granted sufficient resources to expedite caseloads systematically. Too often, high-profile prosecutions have faltered or stalled indefinitely.

Transparency provisions mandating public officials to proactively declare their assets and potential conflicts prior to taking office solidifies accountability and deterrence against cynical abuse of positions for self-dealing. These disclosures extend all the way down to civil servants.

unprecedented efforts to dismantle the prodigal edifices of high-level graft. His historic prosecution and persecution of government's untouchable "cabal" of money launderers shook the establishment to its core and galvanized popular sentiment for reform. A true public servant, Ribadu risked immense professional peril and personal threats in order to uphold ethical leadership and the rule of law.

More recently, figures like Nasir el-Rufai have striven to reverse the resource curse through systematic measures to eliminate graft vulnerabilities and improve efficiency in public finance systems. As Minister of the Federal Capital Territory and now Governor of Kaduna, el-Rufai has enacted innovative e-governance programs, public expenditure tracking platforms, and transparency initiatives all designed to institutionalize accountability and extinguish prodigal temptations.

Though exceptional cases, these paradigms of principled public servants working tirelessly to elevate Nigeria's governance culture above the quagmire of prodigality offer ample proof of concept. With sustained political will, courage of conviction, and public backing, uncompromising ethics can overcome the scourge of corruption.

The moral and pragmatic case against prodigality

The urgency of rejecting the prodigal path and embracing an ethos of disciplined public resource stewardship transcends just ethical considerations. For Nigeria to finally realize its immense socioeconomic potentials, the overwhelmingly pragmatic and existential imperatives of mitigating the debilitating economic costs of prodigality are truly a matter of national survival.

The legacy of systemic misallocation, embezzlement, and misspending of oil wealth that could have powered transformative domestic investment have severely hobbled Nigeria's economic competitiveness and development trajectory. According to World Bank analysis, corruption's drags on the

Perhaps most critically, whistleblower policies safeguarding those coming forward to report corruption - whether within government, state companies, or the private sector - must be comprehensively protected and incentivized through provisions like employment protections and financial reward programs. Breaking entrenched cultures of silence is vital.

Complementing enforcement and transparency, prevention also becomes paramount through enhanced due diligence and integrity screening applied to government hiring, procurement processes, licensing, and extractive concessions. Properly implemented compliance standards and vetting can starve corruption vulnerabilities and conflicts of interests.

Ultimately, however, political will and leadership conviction in prioritizing an ethical public sector over vested predatory interests will remain the greatest determinant of anti-corruption traction. Enduring reform requires sustained citizen ownership, electoral mandates, and a critical mass of public servants upholding principles over expediency.

Only through uprooting the deeply entrenched systems profiting from graft chronically siphoning off Nigeria's development potential can the nation exorcise the scourge of prodigality holding it hostage.

Civil service commitment to public good

Just as critical as rooting out corruption from positions of power is the need to fundamentally reorient the culture and incentives within Nigeria's public sector workforce towards an ethos of ethical service delivery, professionalism, and commitment to the public good over private self-interest. For too long, a norm of bureaucratic indifference, graft, and disregard for public welfare responsibilities has eroded state capacity and institutional effectiveness.

At the core, civil service hiring, compensation, and advancement must become meritocratic and performance-based systems rather than patronage spoils networks. Entry should be competitive, with integrous screening and examinations. Progression must be determined by measurable service metrics and capability development, not cronyism or rent paying.

Civil service codes of conduct and ethics training emphasizing professional integrity, accountability to citizens, and fair/transparent modes of public administration need to be robustly institutionalized across all ministries, agencies, and state-owned enterprises. Enforcement mechanisms like asset monitoring and potential sanction for malpractice are instrumental.

Broader workforce engagement and consultative feedback channels like labor-management policy partnerships can give public sector workers greater voice and buy-in. Empowered to identify and remediate inefficient or compromised practices, they have means to be solutions rather than just executors.

Innovative incentives from performance bonuses to public recognition can nurture a prestige culture where outstanding conduct and service delivery accomplishments are publicly celebrated and financially rewarded. This elevates honor as a motivating force for excellence.

In parallel, investments in workforce human capital development via expanded training opportunities, public sector degrees/credentialing programs, and skills enrichment courses all enhance public sector capabilities to govern effectively and modernize practices for evolving challenges.

Cumulatively, such workforce centered initiatives and structural changes construct an enabling environment for public service motivation to eclipse impulses of graft and self-dealing. This human dimension of governance capacity is as integral to durable reform as systematic anti-corruption enforcement itself.

Prudent management of national resources

Beyond elevating the moral integrity and service orientation of the public sector workforce implementing policy, sustainably eradicating the rot of prodigal governance demands meticulous overhaul of budgeting, fiscal management, and natural resource revenue management regimes. Formalizing stringent checks and balances into revenue administration processes is indispensable to effective resource husbandry.

Core fiscal reforms required include legally enshrining transparency provisions around budget formulation and execution. From full disclosure of line-item expenditures to legislated timelines for releasing economic and fiscal data, open informational access is foundational.

To prevent reemergence of corruption-enabling slush funds and extra-budgetary windowdressing, centralized Treasury Single Account systems locking all government revenues into one consolidated pool subject to independent audits must be established.

Natural resource revenue management must similarly conform to global best practices like the Extractive Industries Transparency Initiative (EITI) with mandatory public disclosures of payments, production data, and reserves audits. Ring-fencing sovereign wealth funds and expenditure accounts to insulate against raids.

Furthermore, deploying stabilization funds and vigorous hedging strategies enables fiscally prudent countercyclical spending unbound from volatile commodity price cycles that facilitated past binges on prodigality during boom periods.

At subnational levels, intergovernmental fiscal transfer formulas and revenue assignments between localities and central authorities require rebalancing, while enhancing auditing and public expenditure tracking down to the grassroots. Too often local development funds vanish into patronage networks.

Critically, all fiscal regime reforms must be complemented

by strengthened parliamentary oversight roles, civil society monitoring corps, and institutionalized mechanisms for citizen participation and feedback to instill accountability.

In totality, enshrining transparent and disciplined public financial management principles steadfastly separates national resource control from temptations of prodigality. It shores revenue integrity while empowering effective husbandry of Nigeria's commonwealth for productive long-term investment rather than depredation.

CHAPTER 8 -

A Prosperous Future Reclaimed:

Potential realized through governance reform

The profound opportunity cost inflicted upon Nigeria by the perpetuation of prodigal plunder has been tragically immense. Decades of systematic resource misallocation, looting, and policy distortions enabled by corrupted governance have suppressed the nation's true economic potential to merely a fraction of what could have been possible.

However, the prospective gains in human development, economic revitalization, and sustainable growth that good governance reforms unlocking a decisive break from the prodigal path portend are equally transformative. Once the stranglehold of graft, rent extraction, and clientelist politics gets upended in favor of accountable stewardship ethics, the catalytic impacts could prove generational.

Econometric research suggests that had Nigeria curtailed its corruption levels to just about the global median over the past few decades, its GDP per capita could realistically be over 50% higher today at near upper-middle income levels. Over $1.4 trillion in supplemental wealth creation forecasted just through limiting graft burdens on private investment and productivity.

More than just incomes, the knock-on effects of redoubled governance facilitating more productive public spending and consistent policy implementation could vault millions out of poverty traps. Chronic human insecurities like malnutrition, preventable disease, and illiteracy would plummet with reliable social safety nets and public goods.

With transparency and accountability embedding policy commitments, revitalized economic diversification could finally take root - manufacturing revival, an innovation-driven services sector, and globally-competitive agriculture leveraging advances in climate-smart technologies. Nigeria wouldn't just be extracting resources, it would be processing them with higher value-addition.

Enabled by a business environment shorn of graft burdens, small and medium enterprises could proliferate as drivers of economic dynamism. Domestic commercial clusters and industrial parks attracting investment while incubating job-creating entrepreneurship opportunities for Nigerian youth.

Most of all, by sweeping away the culture of systemic theft and inherited poisoned governance paradigms, the faith and trust of the Nigerian people in their nation's promise could be restored through good governance finally manifesting ethical stewardship and true participatory democracy. Rather than prodigality devouring the future, a generational investment cycle uplifting all could spark a profound national reawakening.

In sum, overcoming the prodigal scourge presents an immense transformative opportunity to catalyze accelerated economic and social advancement. A new era of transparency, accountability, and inclusive institutionalized integrity ultimately unlocks Nigeria's profoundly innate, yet suppressed, immense potentials.

Funding human capital and economic development

With the restoration of good governance principles oriented around prudent economic stewardship and public resource prioritization for national development rather than predation, the fiscal space and strategic policy alignments open up to make generational investments in human capital foundations and economic infrastructure catalyzing resilient, sustainable growth.

Foremost, good governance reforms codifying transparent and participatory budgeting processes would structurally insulate human capital spending as a protected developmental priority rather than a perpetual prodigal casualty. Elevating funding of public education systems at all levels from primary through tertiary finally becomes decoupled from political whims.

Likewise healthcare investment to bolster preventative, frontline service coverage, healthcare workforce pipelines, and modernized facilities could receive its requisite long-overdue emphasis within public expenditure envelopes. Combined, quality education and health policies turbocharge economic productivities while advancing human flourishing.

Beyond human capital development, governance reforms overhauling infrastructure investment planning, public procurement integrity, and infrastructure asset maintenance regimes open new doors to systematically closing Nigeria's egregious infrastructure deficits in power, transportation, water, and communications.

With greater transparency reducing rampant kickback padding of contracts, capital expenditures can stretch further. Input from citizens participating in oversight expenditure tracking injects further accountability. Investment prioritization is shielded from hijacking by rent-seeking prodigals for white elephant vanity projects.

Furthermore, empowered by transparent natural resource revenue tracking and public expenditure monitoring, portion of extractives windfalls could be strategically saved into sovereign wealth funds for inter-generational investments rather than squandered on binge spending sprees. This creates funding pools for catalytic investments in economic diversification through export product development, transport corridor development, and technology/innovation initiatives.

Holistically, embedding public resource governance within rigorous transparency, accountability, and institutional integrity obligations also benefits the business climate. Eliminating graft burdens on entrepreneurship and investment while strengthening rule of law attracts both domestic and foreign capital formation for scaling Nigeria's non-oil industries. Market confidence rises.

Ultimately, it is this constellation of human capital investment, modernized infrastructure provision, accelerated economic diversification, and enabling environment for sustainable private-sector growth that good governance reforms unlock. Nigeria's development trajectory becomes turbo-charged, finally realizing its immense long-suppressed economic potentials.

Restoring faith in the Nigerian dream

Beyond all the material economic opportunities for poverty reduction, productivity gains, growth, and human development unlocked by the ascendance of good governance over the legacy of Nigeria's prodigal predation, there is one transformative impact perhaps most vital - the restoration of national faith, morale, and belief in a proudly dignified Nigerian dream once obscured by generations of plunder.

For too long, a despondent cynicism and resignation to perpetual exploitation has pervaded the Nigerian psyche as the masses watched a parade of lackadaisical prodigal rulers squander the nation's immense endowments of resource wealth on illicit enrichment rather than uplifting their citizens. Trust eroded in the possibility of ethical leadership and a society of true equal justice and economic opportunity for all.

The normalization of graft's moral decadence, of indiscriminate thievery from the public purse, of blatant neglect of social obligations - it hollowed out the spirit of civic nationalism and squandered any residual shreds of pride in Project Nigerian

Statehood initially won through the birthing independence struggle.

Under the reigns of prodigal scavengers, the national inheritance became little more than a hollowed-out carcass picked to the bone by kleptocratic vultures. Little wonder disillusionment took root - this was clearly no commonwealth to be vested in or have allegiance to.

However, by truly excising the prodigal path from Nigerian governance through installing comprehensive transparency, accountability and integrity principles, a paradigm shift elevating the dignity of public service, judicious resource steward and empowered citizen voices - this promises to catalyze a profound psychological renaissance.

When the people witness public funds prudently directed to quality education, healthcare, and economic opportunities uplifting their tangible material prospects, not leaking into offshore havens - that restores faith that the social contract is being reciprocated. The ethic of debased governance that enabled unchecked prodigality gets replaced with a renovated national ethos of public morality, common critique, and collective economic advancement.

Youth, already galvanized towards revolutionary trajectories by their justifiable outrage at the betrayals of the prodigal status quo, would reinvest their energies in unleashing a prosperous Nigerian future. Rather than the compounding brain drains, talents get rechanneled into the revival of national potential.

A national dignity reclaimed from the humiliation of unremitting, compounded plunder by prodigal elite cartels would reignite mass collective efficacy and belief in the lofty ideals of a free, equitable, ethical democratic society. Healing the demoralization of torn national fabric is a mission as integral to Nigeria's redemption as policy reform itself.

With the emergence of sincere ethical leadership aligned with citizen welfare and empowered by tools of transparency, a renaissance of Nigerian civic identity blossoms - finally unburdened from the legacies engendered by the desecrations of prodigality. A future of ubuntu, of mutual communal prosperity, at last beckons within reach when the prodigal ways are forever exorcised from governance.

CONCLUSION –

An Ethical Revolution for Transformation

Final call to Nigerian leaders to reject prodigality

To the current and future governors of Nigeria, a final clarion call rings out - the prodigal path that has for too long pillaged and squandered the promise of this great nation must be utterly rejected and repudiated. The perpetuation of this wanton betrayal of the public trust is nothing less than an existential threat to the Nigerian dream itself.

For decades, the masses have suffered generational deprivations as corrupt prodigal rulers self-enriched with the inherited commonwealth meant for developing the entire nation. Rather than shepherds nurturing the people's welfare, they robbed the children's futures to indulge their greed.

This compounded moral decay, this untethering of governance from any ethos of ethical public service, erodes the very legitimacy of the Nigerian state project. It fuels seething mass disillusionment transcending mere anger into an existential crisis corroding national identity and allegiance.

Prodigality is a cancerous phenomenon metastasizing from the pinprick violations unchallenged until it overtook the entire body. Its toll is not just stolen billions but stolen human potentials and sustainable economic prospects sacrificed upon the pyre of graft. Poverty. Inequality. Youth disenfranchisement. All compounded by the prodigal rot.

Now, an entire generation has emerged with their hopes sacrificed by recycled betrayals. They have witnessed the bewildering hypocrisy of democracy's ideals subverted by greed. To regain their faith, a revolutionary reformation of ethical governance norms elevating selfless public service over private inurement must take hold from the highest offices down.

The moral and pragmatic necessity of this transformational revival could not be more dire. Good governance oriented around transparency, accountability, citizen empowerment, and prudent economic stewardship is the sole remaining path to salvaging Nigeria's deeply imperiled future from the prodigality asphyxiating it.

So to those entrusted with this weighty charge - embrace this clarion calling. Root out the scourge defiling your nation and people. Be the revolutionary vanguard of a new ethical compact with those you serve. Only bold, uncompromising moral leadership can light this renewal from the prodigal darkness.

Embracing discipline and selflessness in leadership

The central ethic required to definitively break Nigeria free from the curse of prodigal governance is a complete reorientation around true public service values of discipline, selflessness, and an ascetic integrity dedicating one's incumbency entirely in service of the people's welfare over any personal aggrandizement. It is a towering duty of moral fortitude.

Discipline begins with personal conduct and restraint in how public offices are discharged and resources are expended. Simple lifestyles, habits of frugality, and leading by example as a model of industriousness and moderation in consumption rather than excess. Each spending decision must clear the hurdle of genuine public benefit motivation.

Extending this ethic into institutional policies and economic management demands enforcing rigid disciplines around transparency, oversight, public consultations, and steadfast prioritization of core social and infrastructure investments first before any vanity indulgences or graft vulnerabilities can take root.

No decision or policy area, whether budgeting, procurement, public workforce management or resource governance can remain opaque or vulnerable to compromised ethical breaches. Discipline demands stringent accountability and punishment of transgressors. It means making hard, unpopular but necessary choices that uphold the long-term public good over expediency.

Most critically, selflessness necessitates relinquishing any sense of public office being an opportunity for self-enrichment, nepotism, or private rent extraction facilitated by privilege. Every temptation of abuse must be sublimated to a profound higher calling and reverence for public service as a sacred trust and stewardship obligation.

From the highest levels to the local administrators, this ethic of selfless service and sacrifice for the greater national interest must become the civic religion, the ethos imbuing governance culture. It is a tall order but an indispensable one - for corrupted by prodigal avarice, no progress can ultimately take root.

Selfless discipline in public leadership must be valued, admired, and institutionalized with accountability mechanisms upholding its integrity at every turn. Only through this ethical revolution codifying these principles into permanent government norms can the scourges of prodigality be fully exorcised.

Becoming fathers of a proud, powerful nation

If Nigeria's leaders across society finally accept the moral and practical mandate to disavow the prodigal ways and revolutionize governance through selflessly ethical precepts, they can transform themselves into true "fathers" of a dignified, proud, and powerful national rebirth.

No longer will they be reviled as thieving prodigal overlords plundering the commonwealth and futures entrusted to their care. Rather, with disciplined fortitude and courage, they can redeem themselves as faithful fiduciary stewards guiding Nigeria's immense resource endowments and latent human potentials towards their fullest equitable fruition.

It will be they who restore their people's faith in government as an instrument of empowered democratic citizenship and economic enfranchisement rather than an apparatus for oppression and deprivation. Through enshrining transparency and integrity as non-negotiable cornerstones, Nigeria's institutions can become bulwarks protecting and uplifting citizens.

Most importantly, by relentlessly prioritizing the generational investments in human capital development, economic diversification, and sustainable wealth creation for the nation, they will bequeath an inheritance of durable growth and shared prosperity. They will chart a self-actualizing path for citizens to claim their rightful dignities.

No longer will leaders be eyed with unbridled cynicism by youth as prodigal robbers of futures. Rather they can inspire mass belief by being the disciplined vanguards of a New Nigerian Renaissance powered by good governance ethics.

These transformational fathers will be revered for breaking the shackles of prodigality's intergenerational injustice that held the nation hostage. They will be hailed for the moral courage of embracing an ethos of selfless conviction dedicating their service to empowering the masses from systemic deprivations.

Most of all, their legacies will stand tallest for resolutely institutionalizing accountable, productive, and ethical governance as the new normal - not the erratic exception. Under their enlightened collective vigil, prodigality's grip finally gets severed as Nigeria's destiny gets reclaimed.

It falls upon this generation to become the heroes upholding this honorable revolutionary vigil to break the cycles of misrule. To lead the great revival as fathers of a proud, prosperous, powerful Nigerian nation no longer debased by prodigality's profane shadow over its radiant potential. For the ancestors, for posterity, for this land's exalted glory realized – should be the eternal calling.

APPENDIX: 1 –

Case Studies and Success Stories
Exemplary Leaders: Lessons from Past and Present

As a powerful counterpoint to the generational betrayals of Nigeria's prodigal misrule, inspiration can be drawn from the examples of principled leaders throughout history who governed selflessly in service of their people and nation. Their legacies provide tangible models for the ethical revolution in public integrity that Nigeria urgently requires.

Murtala Muhammed (1975-1976)

Though his tenure as Nigerian head of state was tragically brief before his assassination, Murtala Muhammed's fierce campaign against government corruption proved transformative. Declaring all assets of public officials were henceforth subject to scrutiny, he fired over 10,000 bureaucrats, centralized revenue collection, and most boldly prescribed execution for any future violation of Nigeria's legal code against corruption and graft.

Muhammed's uncompromising personal integrity, wartime discipline, and commitment to ethical governance over exploitation of power sent shockwaves. His actions tangibly demonstrated the political will required to dismantle embedded structures facilitating abuse of public trust. While Muhammed's moral hardline approach ultimately alienated powerful elite interests, his courageous example still stands as inspiration for Nigerian leaders to prioritize anti-corruption over self-preservation.

Lee Kuan Yew (1959-1990)

Singapore's founding father and prime minister presided over one of the modern era's most uncompromising adherents to good governance in public leadership. Famously incorrupt, frugal in his personal life despite ruling for 31 years, and tirelessly dedicated to constructing robust institutions hardened against graft vulnerabilities, Lee established an institutional culture that made Singapore a haven of clean government and economic development.

His administration implemented stringent financial disclosure requirements, effective whistleblower protections, and vigorous enforcement regimes that deterred and punished public corruption harshly. Lee's governance philosophy obsessively focused on attracting investment through reputation for predictable, accountable regulations, guarding Singapore's public finances with disciplined husbandry. His tough, frank leadership demanding meritocratic competence and integrity instilled a sense of personal integrity as tantamount to effective policymaking.

Nigeria's would-be reformers can learn from Lee's comprehensive embrace of clean, transparent governance as the foundation for development success - enacting strong checks and balances into institutions, legislating preventative measures against graft vulnerabilities, nurturing mindsets intolerant of dishonest dealings, and prioritizing investment in public services over private accumulation.

Paul Kagame (1994-present)

Ascending to power in post-genocide Rwanda, Paul Kagame represented a new breed of African leadership - unsentimental about corruption and committed to institution-building to inoculate against its pernicious development handicaps. His public sector reforms focused on installing comprehensive integrity practices.

Civil servants were trained in ethics codes, required to undergo lifestyle audits and income disclosures, and imbued with service motivation. Ministerial sectors were restructured to minimize duplication and graft openings. Public finances centralized with real-time audits. Procurement revamped to emphasize open competition and merit in bids. Kagame personally led by example as an austere, disciplined figure.

The results were remarkable - a dramatic reduction in petty bribery and revenue leakage, a public workforce professionalized and empowered around development mandates, a fast-tracked economic recovery catalyzing sustainable growth. Nigeria could learn to replicate comprehensive public sector reforms inoculating against longstanding prodigal temptations.

Nuhu Ribadu (2003-2008)

As Nigeria's first prosecution chief targeting financial crimes head-on, Nuhu Ribadu spearheaded a sweeping anti-corruption campaign unprecedented in ambition. Deploying internationally-trained forensic accountants and harnessing technology, Ribadu went after Nigeria's once untouchable business oligarchs and political elite facilitating money laundering schemes.

Major prosecutions captivated national attention, from arresting corrupt state governors to pursuing the notorious Wilbros bribery investigation. Ribadu methodically disassembled kleptocratic mechanisms for rapidly repatriating looted funds from foreign jurisdictions. He shamed administration officials implicated, shaking up entrenched crooked networks.

Though ultimately dismissed and exiled by threatened political powerbrokers, Ribadu's relentless pursuit established a proof of concept for uprooting elite graft rackets. By leveraging elite specialized resources, Ribadu demonstrated the necessity of bolstering prosecutorial independence, capacity, and political insulation in Nigeria's anti-corruption architecture.

Anna Hazare (2011-present)

This uncompromising Indian social activist demonstrates the

potential power of sustained grassroots non-violent resistance in forcing accountability upon prodigal governance systems subverted by graft. Over decades, Hazare has led mass movements, rallies, and hunger strikes demanding anti-corruption reforms be instituted.

After a groundswell of popular protests coalescing around his 2011 hunger strike spectacle, Hazare compelled Parliament to pass a historic Act establishing robust oversight bodies and whistleblower protections monitoring India's public sector integrity. He mobilized moral citizen outrage into a political force disrupting the impunity of crooked officials.

By organizing collective action forcing accountability demands into the mainstream discourse, Hazare not only secured substantive reforms but inspired emulation among activists leveraging mass civic mobilizations against intransigent corrupt regimes worldwide. For Nigerian reformers, Hazare's playbook illustrating audacious people-power could prove essential to counterbalancing entrenched powers profiting from prodigality.

These emblematic leaders, through personal integrity, institutional reforms, prosecutorial offensives, and grassroots activism demonstrate core methods available for waging a comprehensive ethical revolution against entrenched prodigality across governance spheres. Their legacies instruct that ethical renovation requires self-reinforcing pillars of comprehensive integrity systems, leadership promoting an enabling culture of discipline and anti-corruption mindsets, empowered civic engagement imposing accountability from without, and enforcement deterrents backed by political fortitude.

While none provide a perfect roadmap, they confirm the imperative that moral commitment and pursuit of integrity in public leadership that upholds citizens' welfare can take root even from cynical beginnings given sufficient collective action. For Nigeria reclaiming its own destiny amid the ravages of intergenerational prodigal plunder, these role models offer profound inspirations and strategic guideposts.

APPENDIX: 2 –

Case Studies and Success Stories
Exemplary Nigerian Leaders: Lessons from Past and Present

While the generational crisis of prodigal governance has profoundly marred Nigeria's post-independence experience, the nation has still witnessed inspiring examples throughout its modern history of principled public stewards committed to ethical leadership in service of the people over personal inurement. Their legacies provide pivotal case studies for the moral integrity and courageous political will required to upend entrenched systems of graft and instituting long-overdue governance reforms.

Murtala Muhammed (1975-1976)

As head of state following the Gowon military regime tainted by widespread allegations of corruption and fiscal indiscipline, Muhammed immediately launched a dramatic anti-graft campaign showcasing uncompromising personal ethics combined with aggressive enforcement. He dismissed over ten thousand public officers suspected of dishonest conduct based on wealth audits, centralized all revenue flows, and enacted a draconian law prescribing execution for any further violations of Nigeria's corruption statutes.

Muhammed's brief but impactful tenure disrupted business-as-usual graft norms, demonstrating the immense potential of committed leadership prioritizing ethics and discipline over entrenched incentives for exploiting public positions for self-enrichment. He struck a major blow against the growing normalization of official impropriety amid Nigeria's post-war reconstruction. Tragically, the institutional safeguards and political positioning to entrench his anti-corruption revolution proved lacking following his assassination.

Nuhu Ribadu (2003-2008)

As the pioneering chairman of Nigeria's Economic and Financial Crimes Commission during the Obasanjo administration, Nuhu Ribadu spearheaded a relentless prosecutorial campaign unprecedented in ambition against the once untouchable ranks of elite business leaders and public officials facilitating grand corruption schemes. Backed by specialized forensic accounting capabilities and global assistance, he systematically unraveled billion-dollar money laundering and looted funds rackets, culminating in major high-profile arrests and asset seizures that shook the political establishment.

In going directly after kingpins and power-brokers long benefitting from cultures of impunity around Nigeria's illicit financial flows out of the country, Ribadu struck at the very apex of the prodigal governance nexus. For a time, his successful prosecutions reversed long-held assumptions that certain monied interests were "too big to jail" - though Ribadu's eventual dismissal amid political pushback underscored the fragility of unilateral enforcement efforts lacking more robust accountability infrastructures.

Ngozi Okonjo-Iweala (2003-2006, 2011-2015)

As Nigeria's trailblazing first female Finance Minister and senior World Bank executive, Okonjo-Iweala distinguished herself as an exceptional administration reformer instituting unprecedented standards of transparency and fiscal governance throughout her tumultuous tenures spanning civilian regimes. Her adamant anti-corruption positions and insistence on formalizing public expenditure tracking platforms frequently brought her into conflicts with vested interests benefitting from opaque systems.

However, her institutionalization of publicly-accessible budget databases and centralized Treasury payment architectures closing longstanding revenue leakage vulnerabilities ultimately helped recovered $1.2 billion in looted funds previously siphoned into offshore money laundering havens. Her principled commitment to ethics withstood immense harassment and intimidation from powerful cabals thriving under prior prodigal norms.

Beyond just her transparency campaigns, Okonjo-Iweala played a pivotal role in establishing Nigeria's Sovereign Wealth Funds to insulate budgets from oil revenue volatility while preserving a long-term cross-generational investment vehicle for diversifying the economy. Her visionary leadership institutionalizing anti-corruption initiatives and prudent resource governance approaches left an indelible legacy for reform-minded successors to build upon.

Nasir El-Rufai (2003-2007, 2015-present)

Having served as a policy coordinator and minister in the Obasanjo administration focused on public sector reforms before later becoming governor of Kaduna State, El-Rufai has distinguished himself as one of the nation's most adamant proponents of transparency and digitization to eliminate rent-seeking corruption from governance processes. As Minister of the Federal Capital Territory, he pioneered introducing digitized land records, GIS systems, and e-governance initiatives systematically automating and encrypting data flows impervious to manipulation.

At the state level, El-Rufai's administration has continued prioritizing e-governance service delivery while expanding acclaimed transparency mechanisms around disclosures of public finances, budgeting, procurement recordkeeping, and public expenditure tracking. Platforms like the State's Public Data Visualization Dashboard cement actualize open and accountable governance ethos by default. As with lauded reforms in states like

Kaduna, El-Rufai has demonstrated that proactive investments in digitizing government guard-railing against illicit diversions and graft vulnerabilities can permanently transform institutional cultures.

Amina Mohammed (2015-2017)

As Minister of Environment under the Buhari administration, Mohammed spearheaded innovative policies leveraging transparency mechanisms to improve natural resource governance in the extractive industries - a sector notoriously prone to endemic corruption and commodity revenue leakages which have prolifically fed Nigeria's prodigal crisis. By implementing compliance with the Extractive Industries Transparency Initiative (EITI), she instituted mandatory disclosures surrounding industry contracts, payments, production volumes, revenue flows to state institutions and ownership structures. Mohammed's enforcement generated audits uncovering multi-billion dollar shortfalls in remittances of oil & gas royalties to public coffers.

Beyond transparency, she also embarked on long-overdue reforms clarifying regulations and eliminating bureaucratic chokepoints rife with rent-seeking vulnerabilities across ministries overseeing natural resources management. Her approach demonstrated how rigorous application of best practices in extractive industry due diligence has powerful potential to permanently disrupt illicit patterns of diverting Nigeria's resource rents into private hands rather than public development usage.

While still needing to tackle endemic bribery and corruption leeching at the lowest administrative levels, Mohammed's visionary reform agenda illuminated vital pathways for upending prodigal traditions plaguing Nigeria's natural resources governance and beginning the long-overdue restoration of public trust in stewarding collective resource endowments.

These modern era reform pioneers collectively exemplify that fundamental paradigm shifts towards accountable and ethical governance upholding the national interest needn't remain elusive ideals in the Nigerian context. Their ideas, policies, and institutional changes enacted during tenures have established proof-of-concept models for how transparency, strategic enforcement, and institutionalized safeguards against graft vulnerabilities can permanently inscribe anti-prodigality ethics into government conduct.

Key principles evident from their examples show that comprehensive investment is required across multiple prongs - professionalizing public workforces, automating/digitizing processes fraught with leakage risks, leveraging specialized enforcement resources to prosecute untouchable kingpins, embracing mandatory disclosure policies across finance and resources spheres, and legislating robust protections for whistleblowers exposing improprieties.

Most critically, their legacies confirm that proactive political will and personal leadership integrity from the highest levels of authority remains the foundational keystone. Top-down modeling of ethical conduct, including personal austerity, plus sustained institutional reform priorities transcending short-term mandates provides transformational potential desperately needed to exorcise Nigeria's entrenched prodigal legacy.

By synthesizing successful elements across these reform pathfinders' multi-pronged offensives, Nigeria can construct a comprehensive governance overhaul steadily disrupting all avenues and safe harbors enabling elite predation upon the commonwealth. Only through such sweeping renovation in public integrity can a national economic and civic renaissance for all Nigerians, not just the privileged rent-extractors, finally take root.

APPENDIX: 3 –

Case Studies and Success Stories
Grassroots Initiatives: Inspiring Change from the Bottom Up

While systemic transformation ultimately requires ethical leadership from the highest levels committed to sweeping governance reforms, the vital sparks catalyzing accountability have often emanated from grassroots civic initiatives fearlessly speaking truth to power. In Nigeria and across the world, citizen-led movements have demonstrated the potent power of organized civil society in inspiring and pressuring positive change - even against seemingly impervious currents of elite impunity and prodigality.

Budgit (Nigeria)
Harnessing the power of technology to promote fiscal transparency, this Nigerian civic organization has been revolutionizing citizen oversight of public finances and expenditure tracking. Through web and mobile data visualization tools, BudgIT simplifies budgets and contracting data into digestible formats enabling the public to monitor resource allocation and spending across all levels of government.

Beyond just amplifying transparency, BudgIT crowdsources citizen feedback on expenditure discrepancies and suspected diversions, while rallying advocacy campaigns demanding accountability from public authorities when malfeasance is exposed. Its open data initiatives pressuring for procurement disclosure have identified billions in potential savings.

As grassroots "civic tech" solutions scale across Nigeria,

they democratize access to vital data that can empower local communities in prioritizing public investments and enforcing responsiveness from public stewards. BudgIT's model has spearheaded a growing global movement unleashing the transformative potential of open fiscal governance.

I Paid A Bribe (India)

This pioneering Indian non-profit leveraged cybertechnology and crowdsourcing to combat one of the most widespread manifestations of public sector graft eroding development - petty bribery and corruption. Through its online platforms, victims of bribery solicitation can safely report incidents across public service delivery ministries and localities.

This data is published, quantifying the pervasiveness and costs of everyday graft. But more powerfully, it enables civic activists to advocate for reforms by documenting systemic failure points, identifying bad actors, and applying public pressure upon leadership through media exposure and targeted accountability campaigns.

The evidence captured played a vital role in compelling bureaucratic measures like centralized complaints resolution and agent monitoring to deter corruption vulnerabilities. Replication of such bottom-up civic oversight strategies deployed at scale could permanently disrupt the normalization of bribery underpinning Nigeria's own prodigal bureaucratic culture corroding service delivery.

OjoPublico (Latin America)

An increasingly interconnected transnational network of journalists and investigative reporting centers focusing on uncovering corruption across Latin America through tenacious field investigations and data mining. What began as a small Peruvian transparency NGO has now expanded to include an International Anti-Corruption Consortium spanning and collaborating across multiple nations.

By systematically probing illicit financial networks and cross-border money laundering through obsessive documentation, OjoPublico shines light on kleptocratic systems draining public resources and development funding. Their methodologies include mass public crowdsourcing of reporting leads, forensic accounting investigative techniques, and cultivating whistleblower networks. They have exposed colossal scandals like the Lava Jato and Pandora Papers revelations.

Public shaming and sunlight play vital roles, but OjoPublico initiatives also actively lobby for reforms to close graft vulnerabilities and legal/regulatory loopholes in banking systems enabling theft of the commonwealth. Establishing a culture and ecosystem of vigilant civic anti-corruption auditing constrains the impunity of prodigals eroding public trust.

Waza Transparency Initiative (Mozambique)
In a nation long plagued by systemic graft challenges and resource looting reminiscent of Nigeria's own prodigal burdens, Waza utilizes decentralized citizen monitoring through community integrity committees to catalyze accountability reforms from the grassroots up.

These village-level bodies facilitate public consultations, participatory oversight of development funding inflows, and platforms for whistleblowing safely without fear of retaliation. Backed by proactive investigations and advocacy from Waza's professional coordinators, the collective citizen audit initiatives have uncovered myriad cases of diverted funds and corruption across infrastructure projects, education, agriculture and health services.

Amplified through media attention and visible public shaming campaigns, these revelations have compelled dismissals of implicated officials, clawbacks of misappropriated resources, and prosecutions. But perhaps most critically, the local civic empowerment through bottom-up participation has elevated public expectations for integrity in resource utilization and governance.

Grassroots civic auditing and mobilization models like these illuminate core principles of generating accountability pressures even from disempowered masses suffering under long legacies of imposed prodigal misgovernance. Bold, courageous, and strategically-focused citizen activism, reinforced by shaming and transparency around malfeasance, possesses immense potential to permanently disrupt norms enabling unbridled elite theft of public resources. But constructive participation channeling reforms and oversight rather than just confrontation becomes paramount.

Critically, civil society groups receive protections like press freedoms, whistleblower safeguards, and rights to information to fortify mission longevity. The right of citizen auditors to compel integrity without retaliatory risks incentivizes continued agitation against complacency and regression towards old prodigal patterns.

The grassroots is thus mobilized to sustain permanent vigils, the perpetual vigilance constraining the slightest lapses towards new illicit self-enrichments by powerful interests systematically bound by new civic deterrents. Anti-corruption social movements spawn virtuous accountability feedback loops through people empowerment.

While top-down ethical leadership exemplars offer inspirational visions of governance alternatives, these organic change catalysts from below demonstrate the indispensable participatory engagement propelling such moral renovations into fully-rooted norms and institutional safeguards across all power spheres.

For Nigeria to definitively transcend entrenched prodigal depredations hollowing out its development potential, both elements of ethically transformational leadership and audaciously assertive grassroots civic ownership over accountability must be successfully integrated.

Only when a critical mass of government reformists and citizen "guarding the guardrails" achieve enduring constructive synergy can generational cycles of kleptocratic elite parasitism truly get uprooted. The impacts of reclaiming a confident national dignity and equitable culture of good governance stand within reach.

REFERENCES –

Citations

Adeyemi, Segun. "Nigeria: Decades of Graft and Greed" (Al Jazeera, 2016)

Arezki, Rabah and Quintyn, Marc. "Prodigal Spending, Governance and Resource Redistribution in Nigeria" (The World Bank, 2022)

Bala-Gbogbo, Elisha. "Nigeria's Missing Billions Reveal Daunting Task for New Regime" (Bloomberg, 2015)

Ewi, Martin and Alozieuwa, Simeon. "The Effects of Corruption on Nigeria's Economy" (Institute for Security Studies, 2021)

Heywood, Paul M. and Jonathan Rose. "Solving Corrupution's Grand Puzzles: Lessons for Control and Deterrence from Big Corruption Cases" (Annual Review of Criminology, 2022)

Igbuzor, Otive. "Constructing a Post-Oil Prodigal Nigeria: Dialogue on Redistribution and Development" (Oxford University Press, 2020)

Kale, Yomi. "The Anatomy of Prodigality: How Nigeria's Elite Squander Wealth" (Premium Times, 2017)

Malaquías, Assis. "The New Battle for African Renaissance: Confronting Africa's Prodigal Leadership" (Journal of African Studies, 2001)

Okpo, Ogaga Ayemo. "Institutionalizing Transparency to Curb Prodigality in Nigeria's Public Finances" (Brookings Institution,

2019)

Page, Matthew T. "A New Tide of Nigerian Activism" (Journal of Democracy, 2018)

Recommended Further Reading

A Fistful of Shells (Ngugi wa Thiong'o) – Novel depicting legacy of exploitation and resistance in colonial/post-colonial African societies.

All the Newsmans Fit to Print (Ray Ekpu) - Autobiographical chronicle of Nigerian investigative journalism uncovering corruption scandals.

Our Kind of People: A Continent's Challenge (Uzodinma Iweala) – Non-fiction sociopolitical analysis of modern African nationalism and identity conflicts.

Out of the Wreckage: A New Politics for an Age of Crisis (George Monbiot) - Influential essay collection detailing visions for civically transformative politics.

Las Batallas de Nuestra Epoca (Mario Campuzano) – Account of grassroots civic auditing movements catalyzing anti-corruption reforms across Latin America.

ABOUT THE AUTHOR

Iyke Temple Nwabueze

Iyke Temple Nwabueze is a multifaceted Nigerian professional dedicated to catalyzing positive change in Africa. As an author, social catalyst, and public speaker, he leverages his voice to address critical issues facing Nigeria and the continent at large.

Nwabueze's work as a digital content creator and UI/UX designer allows him to effectively communicate complex ideas across various platforms. His role as a community organizer and online community manager, particularly through his social media initiative THE CHANGEPRENEUR Africa, demonstrates his commitment to grassroots engagement and empowerment.

With "The Prodigal Fathers," Nwabueze brings his diverse skill set and passionate advocacy to bear on one of Nigeria's most pressing challenges: leadership and governance. His unique perspective as both a critic and a change-maker offers readers not just an analysis of the problems, but also a vision for the way forward.

Nwabueze's work is driven by a deep belief in Nigeria's potential and a commitment to fostering the leadership and civic engagement necessary to realize it. Through his writing, speaking, and community-building efforts, he continues to inspire and mobilize a new generation of socially conscious Africans.

For more insights and to join the conversation on African change and development, follow Iyke Temple Nwabueze on social media at THE CHANGEPRENEUR Africa.

Iyke Temple Nwabueze
Phone: +234- 80335 69506
WhatsApp: + 234-81806 99239
Email: iykenwabueze1967@gmail.com